THE *Living* TREE

ACKNOWLEDGEMENTS

So many sources — publications and websites — were employed in researching, writing and illustrating this book. Many published works were consulted — several of my own earlier books, including my *All About* series (New Holland) proved invaluable, as did my old friend Andrew Crowe's excellent *Which?* series (Penguin), and *Field Guide to New Zealand's Native Trees* by John Dawson and Rob Lucas (Craig Potton). Periodicals such as *New Zealand Geographic* and plenty of other publications were handy for interesting little factoids picked up here and there. Websites of various organisations proved very helpful, too — including Te Ara, Department of Conservation, iNaturalistNZ, The New Zealand Herpetological Society — and Wikipedia was a great source of information about the facts, figures and oddities of the world's trees. And lastly, thanks to JSTOR for featuring the tree photograph which inspired the book's cover painting.

Thank you, all.

Dave

Published in 2025 by David Bateman Ltd
Unit 2/5 Workspace Drive, Hobsonville, Auckland 0618, New Zealand
www.batemanbooks.co.nz

ISBN 978-1-77689-133-7

Illustrations: Dave Gunson
Cover design: Alice Bell and Dave Gunson
Book design: Alice Bell and Dave Gunson
Printed in China by Toppan Leefung Printing Ltd

DAVE GUNSON

THE *Living* TREE

A NEW ZEALAND HABITAT

CONTENTS

INTRODUCTION

Is there more to a tree than it being 'just a tree'? Can it support and interact with other life? Most might think of birds nesting in its branches, or bees visiting its flowers, but probably not much more than that.

But if you look very closely, you'll rarely find a more complex and diverse 'contained' living environment than that which can sometimes be found in and around a single tree.

No tree ever lives in isolation — untouched by the natural world around it. A mature tree, whether it's a forest giant or a small garden tree, can be like a great wildlife 'apartment building' with its own unique living community of animals, plants and fungi. There are many permanent residents and plenty of visitors coming and going — some come to see their relatives, or to hunt out others to prey on them. There are places to raise young, to gather food, to hide from predators, or to simply shelter from the weather.

Plenty of opportunities for all sorts of small visitors, backpackers, diners, squatters, guests . . . and hunters.

This book is divided into a typical tree's three main sections — the roots and ground; the trunk; and the branches and leaves.

Each is quite distinct in its nature and in the range of organisms that live in and around it, and all are well worth a closer look.

TREES — RĀKAU

Trees are essential for our survival. Through their leaves, they absorb carbon dioxide from the atmosphere, and produce oxygen, which we humans (and other animals) need to breathe. It's believed that a single mature tree can produce a year's supply of oxygen for ten people in just a single season. While much more than half of all the Earth's oxygen comes from tiny plants — called phytoplankton — found in the oceans, and open grasslands, trees contribute a very healthy 28%.

Although large members of the plant family — such as some early forms of tree ferns and primitive tree-like species — have existed for about 400 million years or more, trees that we would recognise today began to evolve about 350 million years ago.

After flowering plants, trees have become one of the most diverse types of plant in the world. There are nearly 74,000 different species, and scientists believe that there are still thousands more yet to be properly identified. There are lots of them, too — about 3 trillion in total around the world. That's several times more than the number of stars in our own Milky Way galaxy (100–400 billion stars).

Trees have adapted and thrived in all sorts of environments — from lush and vast tropical forests and comfortable temperate regions to the harsh, hot savannah and desert plains to high alpine and icy regions . . . and even in swamps and marshes.

Nearly all trees have the similar basic structure of a root system, trunk and leafy branches.

The roots have two main jobs — to provide stability by securing the tree in the ground, and by drawing food from the earth. Roots are usually widely spread and each grows smaller and smaller rootlets, which

end in fine root-hairs that extract nutrients and water from the soil. This moisture is drawn up through the trunk into the branches and leaves, through a series of very fine, tube-like, woody tissues.

As a tree grows, the trunk becomes thicker and taller, to bring the branches higher so that the leaves can reach open sunlight. The trunk develops a hard outer cover (bark) to protect the softer, live wood inside.

Eventually, the upper trunk divides into branches on all sides. The leaves borne on the branches produce more food for the tree by a process called photosynthesis. The leaves can absorb energy from light, and also take in carbon dioxide. They can then produce oxygen, and provide the sugars that the tree needs to survive and grow.

Deciduous trees — mostly in cooler climates — will shed their leaves during colder or drier months. As their growing slows during those periods, the leaves are shed to save energy. Evergreen trees replace their leaves gradually, so always have full foliage. Evergreens favour warmer climates and rainforests, though both types can be found together around most of the world.

Deciduous trees reproduce by means of pollination — just like a flowering plant in your garden. Bees and other insects, or even wind, will complete the necessary fertilisation by carrying pollen from one tree's flower to the flower of another tree of the same species. Seeds are then produced and released. Evergreen trees don't produce flowers or seeds in the same way. Many grow cones, which produce pollen. The pollen is released and taken by the wind to fertilise another tree. When conditions are right, the new seeds are dispersed, and more trees begin to grow.

DOWN AROUND THE ROOTS

What's going on down there? A first glance, not very much at all. Often, all we can see is the first widening at the base of the trunk where the main roots begin. But there's a great deal that's unseen. The complex root system of many trees can almost mirror the great spread of branches at the top of the tree. The soil around the root system can be rich in nutrients, from the decayed fallen leaves and other materials that have accumulated. This material, plus the growth of roots and water movement, sometimes changes the nature of the soil, and underground hollows and gaps may well appear, providing opportunities for exploitation by animals, plants and fungi.

While most trees have their roots under the ground, some have roots that rise up clear of the ground or grow down to the ground from the branches.

Mangrove roots can take nutrients from the muddy waters in which they grow, but they also need to take in oxygen, which those salty, marshy soils mostly lack. The main roots send up 'breathing roots' vertically, clear of the water's surface.

Banyan trees can grow roots from their branches (called prop roots), which can then anchor in the ground and develop into strong branch-like supports. More and more are added as branches grow outward and can result in a tree with a great forest labyrinth of vertical trunk-like roots.

Mushrooms — Harore

Mushrooms are one of many types of fungus that grow in company with trees. The decaying leaves, fallen branches and other plant material around the base of the trunk provide ideal growing conditions. The fungus grows as a mass of very fine threads through the soil, and when they grow to the surface, they produce the reproductive body — the mushroom — which will then release spores for new growth. Fungi threads can attach themselves to the root tips, and an exchange of nutrients takes place — the fungus can take carbohydrates from the root, and the root can receive nitrogen and phosphate from the fungi. Mushrooms growing directly on exposed roots or on the tree trunk are usually a sign that the tree is infected and unhealthy.

Some mushroom species may associate themselves with specific tree types; the grey-brown *Amanita* species shown here is often found around the base of mānuka and southern beech trees, and the 7cm violet pouch (or king's pouch) fungus can be seen growing from the leaf litter by beech trees. A scarlet cup fungus can be seen in the leaf litter by miro trees.

There are around 22,000 species of fungi in New Zealand, and an estimated 6 million species worldwide.

Trapdoor Spider

While many species of spider will build webs or traps with their silk, or roam freely to hunt prey, some prefer to stay hidden below ground. The trapdoor spider can excavate tunnels up to 30cm deep, where they lie in wait for their victims to pass by. Trapdoor spiders in open country construct a hinged lid for their tunnels, but most of those in the forest leave them open and lidless. The tube tunnel and its opening are lined with silk, and when the spider detects the touch and vibration of a passing insect, it rushes out to grab it and haul it back down the tube. They're large spiders — about 30mm in body length, or more — and there are over 40 native species in New Zealand. They are long-lived, too; some may live up to 20 years.

Despite their size, these spiders still have enemies, especially the 25mm-long large, black hunting wasp — ngaro wīwi — which hunts trapdoor spiders and their close relatives, the tunnelweb spiders (see page 24). If the wasp can get into the tube or burrow, it paralyses the spider with its sting and takes it back home for its larvae to eat, or it sometimes takes over the spider's tunnel as a new food-stocked home.

Slaters — Pāpapa

If there's rotting wood or decaying leaves in the damp and dark spaces around the roots near the tree base — or even fallen fruit — there are sure to be slaters, also known as woodlice. There are about 36 species in New Zealand, in forests, parks and gardens, and most measure about 1cm in length. They aren't insects but belong to the crustaceans, a group of animals that includes shrimp, crabs and lobsters. Slaters have seven pairs of legs while insects have three pairs. Because they excrete ammonia, they don't have many predators — but the aptly-named slater spider finds them tasty enough to hunt them out.

Brown Wolf Spider

This small spider — body length about 9mm — hides under bark, rotting logs or damp leaf litter in the forest during the day, and mostly comes out at night to hunt and chase down its insect prey. Like its daytime relative, the garden wolf spider, the female brown wolf spider carries her egg sack with her as she roams. And when her 100-or-so young hatch, they ride on their mother's back for a few days before becoming independent and leaving home.

There are about 27 species of wolf spider in New Zealand, and about 2200 around the world.

Giant Centipede p23
Tree Wētā p23
Black Tunnelweb Spider p24
White-Tailed Spider p24
Nīkau Moth p24
Red Admiral Butterfly p25
Kānuka Longhorn Beetle p22
Huhu Beetle p22
Exquisite Carpet Moth p21
North Island Lichen Moth p21
Bag Moth p20
Cicada p20
Moss p15
Kauri Snail p27
Kiekie p16
Bush Lawyer p18
Veined Slug p27
Lichen p15
Bracket Fungi p14
Clematis p17
Bumblebees p13
Ants p12
Click Beetles p11
Cosmopolitan Ground Beetle p12
Mushrooms p8
Brown Wolf Spider p9
Earthworms p11
Cicada Nymphs p11
Native Bush Cockroach p10
Slaters p9
Trapdoor Spider p9
Millipede p10
Soil Centipede p10

Kōkako p43
Silvereye p42
Kererū p44
Yellow-Crowned Parakeet p45
Morepork p46
Little Shag p47
Bat p47
Grey Warbler p42
Blackbird p40
Tūī p41
Kākā p46
Forest Gecko p39
Elegant Gecko p39
Shore Skink p38
Mānuka Chafer Beetle p35
Praying Mantis p35
Common Blue Butterfly p36
Fantail p40
Giant Wētā p36
Two-Spined Spider p37
Nursery Web Spider p37
Flower Longhorn Beetle p34
Lemon Tree Borer p34
Gum Emperor Moth p33
Cabbage Tree Moth p33
Leafminer Moth p33
Stick Insect p32
Flower Spider p37
Red Mistletoe p29
Easter Orchid p29
Drooping Spleenwort p29
Honeydew p30
Aphids p31
Ladybirds p31
Old Man's Beard Lichen p28
Perching Lily p28
Honeybee p32
Rata p19
Rifleman p27
Giraffe Weevil p26
Elephant Weevil p26
Pūriri Moth p25
Climbing Plants p16

Millipede — Weri Mano

There are several hundred millipede species in New Zealand, and all feed on decaying vegetation and rotting wood. They can be as small as 2mm in length or as long as 3–5cm. They're usually coloured in shades of brown, from the palest to near black. Unlike centipedes, they are slow walkers, and if disturbed cannot defend themselves other than curling up into a tight spiral. Many can secrete a foul-smelling fluid to deter attackers.

The name 'millipede' implies a thousand legs, but no millipede can actually boast that number, even though they have two pairs of legs to each body segment — centipedes have only one pair per segment.

Most tree roots grow within about 1–2m of the surface, though many can go deeper to follow necessary moisture in the ground. The greatest depth measured of tree roots is 120m, grown by a wild fig tree in the Echo Caves in South Africa.

Soil Centipede — Weri

There are many species of small soil centipedes in New Zealand, and they usually measure between 2–5cm in length. Their two front legs are adapted into poisonous gripping claws. Smaller species are harmless to humans, but larger individuals can administer a painful nip with their claws. All are predators, and mostly seek out insects and their larvae, and larger centipedes can even take on small worms and native snails. In turn, they are eaten by beetles, spiders, birds and even bigger centipedes.

They avoid daylight and roam through loose soil, in the gaps under stones and leaf-litter, and in rotten logs. They can live for several years.

Native Bush Cockroach — Papata/Kokoroihe

There are about 15 native species of these flat-bodied, fast-running insects. Most are about 15mm long. Unlike several introduced species, none of them are pests in houses — they all prefer natural environments. Cockroaches are one of nature's hardiest survivors — they can survive for a couple of weeks without water, and for several months without food. Lifespans of different species can be anything between 6 months and almost 2 years.

They can be found in the dark, damp areas of leaf-litter, under stones, in rotting wood and under tree bark, where they forage for organic materials of all sorts — they especially like leaf litter fungus and can chew and digest dead wood. Even though the cockroach can give out a foul acidic smell, it doesn't deter predators such as larger centipedes, beetles, spiders, rats and mice. Even a praying mantis finds them tasty.

Cicada Nymphs — Matua Kihikihi

The female cicada lays her eggs in tree bark or in plant stems. When the tiny nymphs hatch, they drop down and burrow into the soil — around 40cm or more below the surface — where they attach themselves to the tree's finer roots to feed on sap.

Being so small, they are easy prey for roaming ants and beetles, and may even die from a fungal infection called vegetable cicada. The fungus eats away at the nymph until there's almost nothing left, and then sends out a white fruiting stem to the surface to release its spores — just like a mushroom. Those nymphs that survive can live and thrive underground for several years — moulting old skin several times and growing larger — before emerging from the soil, and climbing back up the tree, for their final moult to become an adult cicada (kikihi) (see page 20).

Click Beetles — Tūpanapana

The larvae of these beetles (called wireworms) live underground for many years, feeding on fine roots and preying on small animals such as cicada nymphs, and other insect larvae. The adult beetles roam through rotting vegetation, soil and bark seeking prey. Some click beetles favour the sap from trees. They gain their name from a special joint under the belly, which they can 'click' or 'pop' (the noise is quite audible) to send them in a 30cm-long (or high) jump to evade predators. If the beetle lands upside-down, it can 'pop' again to right itself.

There are about 135 species in New Zealand, and most are about 10–15cm in length.

Earthworms — Noke

There are over 200 different species of earthworms in New Zealand, nearly all of them are native. They live within the top few centimetres of soil and eat dead leaves and plant debris, and the faeces they excrete is rich in nutrients, which enriches the soil, and in turn helps to give tree roots the food they need. The movement of worms through the soil helps to bring air and water into the soil, too. Earthworms can be found anywhere there is soil — in gardens, pastures and forests. These creatures are both male and female but need to mate with another earthworm to produce eggs. The tiny worms that hatch look like miniatures of their 'parents', and simply grow until they reach adult size — usually anything between 20–35mm in length, depending on the species. The rarely seen giant Northland worm — living up to 3m below the ground in forests — can grow to 1.5m in length. Earthworms can live for between 2–8 years.

Cosmopolitan Ground Beetle — Pāpapa

This 1.5cm long insect is typical of the more than 400 species of ground beetle in New Zealand. Both the larvae and the adult beetle have strong jaws to actively hunt out prey through soil, leaf litter and rotting logs. These beetles can climb up tree trunks to hunt for food, and some can even prey on native snails. Larger species can give a very powerful bite to a human finger, and many give off a foul-smelling odour, earning themselves the Māori name of kurikuri (dog-like).

All ground beetles have a similar appearance, having mostly flat and shiny metallic black or dark brown strongly grooved bodies.

Some tree roots can be used for food, or even beer. Early Māori often cooked the roots and new shoots of the cabbage tree — tī kōuka — and Captain Cook's crew, early European settlers and missionaries managed to make rum and beer from the roots.

Ants — Pōpokorua

The crevices and nooks around and under tree roots are ideal places for ants to establish their nests, and carpenter ants will build nests in rotting logs or even within a tree's bark. New Zealand has about 11 native species of ants, and the most common is the 3mm-long Southern Ant, which nests in spaces under stones or roots as well as in rotting logs. The large native ant is New Zealand's biggest native species and measures up to 10mm in length. It's found in the rotting logs of North Island forests, and feeds on other insects.

A colony usually comprises one or more egg-laying queens, hundreds of male drones and tens of thousands of workers. Queen ants can live for 10–15 years, and workers for less than half that time. Workers explore their surroundings to find food to bring back to the nest. Lines of ants can be seen going up and down the tree's trunk as they seek out seeds, small insects and their eggs, and the honeydew secreted by aphids and scale insects — and some will grow an edible fungus in the colony's nest. They follow a chemical trail of their own making as they travel, and they touch or examine each other as they pass to ensure that no intruders from another colony have joined the line. Depending on the species, ants can bite with strong jaws, administer a sting, or spray formic acid to repulse attackers.

Known simply as 'That Wānaka Tree', a solitary willow growing in the cold waters of Lake Wānaka in the South Island, is probably the most photographed tree in New Zealand. Its image is visible widely online. It's thought the tree began life about 80 years ago as a fencepost cut from a nearby willow tree — but then the fencepost took root and grew.

Bumblebee — Pī Rorohū

Bumblebees were first introduced into New Zealand from England in the 1880s, to help pollinate clover flowers, because the tongues of the previously introduced honeybees were not long enough to reach the flower's pollen. There are now four species here, and usually measure about 2.5cm in body length.

Unlike honeybees, bumblebees live in quite small colonies — often just a few hundred individuals instead of many thousands. Bumblebees do not construct complex hives but make use of crevices and spaces between tree roots, under rocks or thick undergrowth.

Instead of honeycombs, they live in a jumbled collection of small waxy 'pots' and cells to house their eggs, larvae, pollen and nectar. Although it's a haphazard environment, it's well maintained — all rubbish, debris and even dead bees are removed from the colony to keep it clean and hygienic.

Like their honeybee cousins, a single queen bee rules the colony, and she alone lays eggs in the individual cells, where the growing young are tended to and fed by the other bees.

Bumblebees are not as aggressive as honeybees but can administer a sting if unduly disturbed. And unlike the honeybee, the bumblebee's sting is not barbed, but smooth; so, it can sting several times.

Bumblebees have a short lifespan. While the queen can live for a year or more — enough time to rest during winter, and then start a new colony — the worker bees may only live for a few short weeks. If a queen dies, the workers select one of the larvae to be fed royal jelly (a super nutritious substance produced by 'nurse' bees) and become the new queen.

New Zealand also has about 40 species of solitary bees. Some are dark-coloured and hairy, and others look very similar to hive bees, with orange and black bands or markings. They don't live in groups, but instead live alone in underground tunnels with chambers, where the female lays her eggs and stores nectar and pollen for the emerging larvae. They are flower pollinators, but do not make honey.

Most species are between 5–12mm in body length.

UP AND DOWN THE TRUNK

The trunk is the tree's main highway for residents and visitors, and also a sort of natural apartment block. Folds in the bark, crevices and holes all provide opportunities for animals and plants to make a home. As the tree grows, it develops its own individual and unique character — there might be scars left in the bark where branches have fallen, or twists and turns in the trunk as it has grown up and around other trees or landforms.

Tree trunks can differ greatly from species to species. Some trees, such as pōhutukawa and pūriri, may develop multiple spreading trunks close to the ground, or even from ground level. Others may grow a single clean and straight trunk — like tītoki and tānekaha — before the branches appear.

There's a great variety in the nature of tree bark, too. It can be deeply folded and convoluted, ridged or smooth. But no matter the nature of the tree and its bark, visitors and settlers always arrive, to make their homes — both on and in the trunk.

Bracket Fungi — Pūtawa

There are many forms of bracket fungi in New Zealand. They can be seen on dead or living trees, sometimes quite high up on the trunk. The largest may reach over 60cm wide and well over 10cm thick. Some have even been recorded at widths exceeding 1m. They can become as hard and unyielding as the tree from which they draw their nutrients. While other forms of fungi — like mushrooms — may live for only a few days or weeks before collapsing and disappearing, some bracket fungi can live for up to 15–20 years. They can appear in a range of colours — dull browns or greys, or even multi-coloured. The Artist's Porebracket has a very dark surface which is easily scratched to reveal a pale surface underneath — ideal for trampers' graffiti. Clusters of smaller — 6cm — orange or grey bracket fungi can often be seen on tree trunks, too.

Bracket fungi were sometimes used by early Māori as fire starters, or for transporting smouldering embers.

Several trees vie to have the greatest trunk circumference. A Montezuma cypress tree called Arbol del Tule (The Tree of Tule) in Santa Maria del Tule (the town was named after the tree) near Oaxaca in Mexico measures about 35m around. Boabab trees in Limpopo, South Africa have been variously measured to have girths of 40–47m. Both the cypress and the boabab trees have complex, buttressed trunks, so measurements often vary.

Lichens — Pūkohu

Lichens are a form of compound plant called a lichenised fungus. This is a union of a fungus and an alga (a very simple plant). The alga supplies the fungus with sugars through photosynthesis, and the fungus gives the alga nutrients and water in return, and both contribute to give the structure some strength.

The three main types to appear on tree trunks are foliose lichens (grey-green and leaf-like), fruticose lichens (grey green, raised and bushy) and crustose (rough, mostly flat and circular in nature — variously grey, green, yellow-orange, black or white).

Lichens can appear on all sides of the tree trunk, but generally prefer the side facing away from the sun, which is often slightly damper than the sunlit side. Contrary to popular belief, lichens do no harm to trees.

There are over 2000 lichen species in New Zealand, and possibly 18,000–24,000 around the world. Lichens are very slow-growing, and some can survive for hundreds of years.

The greatest trunk girth ever measured was that of the Hundred Horse Chestnut, which grows on a slope of Mt Etna in Sicily, Italy. In 1790, its girth was said to be 57.9m — it would take about 40 men, holding hands with arms outstretched, to encircle it. Since that time, the trunk has split into three main parts, although they all still share the same root system. The tree is believed to be about 4000 years old.
By comparison, the circumference of our 'widest' kauri — Te Matua Ngahere — is just 16.41m.

Moss — Pūkohu/Kohukohu

Mosses have been around for over 400 million years — that's probably about 40 million years before modern, 'true' woody-stemmed trees evolved. There are about 500 species in New Zealand, and while most only grow from a few millimetres to a couple of centimetres in height, our forests are home to the world's tallest free-standing moss Dawsonia — which can reach 60cm in height.

As with lichens, moss on the bark does no harm to the tree, and they also favour the damper side of the trunk. It appears in clumps and mats, often spreading up from the base of the tree, climbing and nestling in the cracks and depressions in the tree's bark. Mosses don't produce flowers or seeds as 'higher' plants do but they reproduce by releasing spores.

Climbing Plants — Akaaka

Plants that grow on other plants are called epiphytes. There are many species of vines and plants which will grow from the ground and attach themselves to tree trunks for support, using twisting and twining stems and tendrils to secure themselves. Some are called shade epiphytes, which remain low on the trunk, and others are sun epiphytes, and these grow high into the tree's branches and crown, where there is generally more natural light. Many of the shade climbers are ferns, and the thread fern (shown here) — pānako — is a typical member of the group. As the thread fern begins its climb from the forest floor, the leaves are about 10cm long, with rounded leaflets. As the fern grows upward and branches out, the leaves lengthen to about 35cm, with narrow, pointed leaflets.

Climbers such as these can ascend 5–10m or more up the tree trunk.

Kiekie

One of the most obvious and abundant tree climbers is the kiekie. This climber is the only New Zealand member of a tropical form of *Pandanus* — a woody-stemmed climbing vine, known as a liana. It's a vigorous grower — it puts out strong roots, which attach themselves to the trunk, and sends more down to the ground to reinforce its position. The result can be untidy masses of descending roots and bunches of spreading leaves — often almost obscuring the host tree entirely all around. Able to live for 20–100 years, the stem of a mature kiekie can almost equal the thickness of a man's arm. Kiekie will climb well, often up into a tree's crown 30m or more above the ground. The leaves can measure over a metre in length, which early Māori have found useful in many applications — for making woven mats and tukutuku panels, rain capes, baskets, fishing traps and whare mats. The male plant produces brown stamen (pollen-laden stems) that are surrounded by fleshy white 'leaves' known as tāwhara to Māori, who found them sweet and tasty to eat. It has a peach-like flavour, and the pulp has sometimes been fermented to be made into a strong drink.

Tree bark can be everything from very thin, to very, very thick. The redwood tree Mill Creek Giant near Crescent City, California has bark measured at 45.7cm thick. Some birch trees and the aptly named paperbark maple tree have bark so thin that it can simply be stripped away like paper. The New Zealand tree, fuschia — kōtukutuku — has an orange-brown papery bark that can be peeled off in strips. Most trees in New Zealand have a bark thickness of anywhere between 0.5–5cm. Generally, the larger the tree, the thicker the bark will be.

Clematis — Puawānanga

Highly regarded as a sacred flower by Māori, this climbing vine is renowned for the displays of beautiful and scented large white flowers (up to 8cm across) it produces in spring. Headdresses made from the flowering stalks are sometimes worn by women on special occasions, such as in times of mourning.

The leaf stalks will twine themselves around anything they touch — trunks, branches and twigs — to climb high into the host tree's canopy. The nectar of the flowers is sought by bees and tūī, and kōkako will eat the entire flower — while kēruru prefer to eat the leaves. Like kiekie, the clematis has a long life span — up to 100 years.

There are several other native species of clematis, but they usually have smaller, creamy-yellow flowers. An introduced climbing clematis — called old man's beard because of the abundance of fluffy white seed heads it produces — was introduced here from Europe in the 1900s, and has become a problem in some forests, as it outgrows and smothers other plants, preventing new native growth.

Tree bark has been used for a wide variety of purposes by humans for thousands of years — for medicine, food, clothing, baskets and even for making canoes. Many trees' inner barks contain chemical compounds useful in treating all manner of bodily illnesses and complaints. The bark of the Pacific yew tree produces a compound commonly used in the treatment of several forms of cancer. The bark of cork trees — a type of oak — is regularly harvested for many uses: stoppers for wine bottles, mats, paper and packaging, and the insides of cricket balls.

It's possible to make bark 'flour' for baking bread from many species of birch and pine trees, and cinnamon bark is used as a popular spice around the world.

The easily stripped outer bark of tōtara trees was used by early Māori for making capes, baskets, torches, splints for limbs, baskets and mats. Mānuka bark was similarly employed. The bark of the hīnau tree was often used to make food baskets and containers, and a black dye or ink could also be made from the bark. The charcoal resulting from burning rimu bark and timber produced a good pigment for tattooing.

Climbing vines

Bush lawyer — tātarāmoa — gets its name from the backward-facing thorns on the stems and undersides of the leaves which catch and tug at the skin or clothing of trampers, pulling them to a sharp halt. And those same hooks help the plant to secure itself and climb to the tree's canopy. It produces edible berries, similar to those of its distant cousin, the blackberry, which are taken by geckos and birds.

The supplejack — kareao — often loses its grip on its chosen tree, and collapses in a tangled heap to the forest floor, from where it will eventually make another attempt. The stems can grow upwards from the ground at about 5cm per day, twisting slowly in an anticlockwise direction, searching for the next support to cling to. The clusters of small red berries are a popular food for native birds, such as kererū and kākā. Where supplejack is common in the forest, passage by humans can be almost impossible. The fallen vines were useful to early Māori for lashings in fencing and building and making bird cages and baskets. The Māori name means 'forest whip'.

New Zealand passionfruit — kōhia — is our only climbing vine that sends out curling tendrils to catch and encircle the tree's outcroppings and branches to secure its ascent. It produces small — 2.5cm — fruit that are favoured by kererū, kākāriki and tūī.

New Zealand jasmine — kaihua — is a vigorous climber. It can climb high into trees, and often gets complicated and twined around itself as it ascends. The thick and thin vines were put to many uses by Māori — for use in building house frameworks and securing fences. The thickly clustered flowers have a very sweet perfume.

Though similar in appearance, it should not be confused with the common garden variety of jasmine that's been introduced from China and has become a forest pest by crowding out native species.

New Zealand Passionfruit

Bush Lawyer

The title of rarest tree in the world must go to our own Three Kings kaikōmako, or kaikōmako manawatāwhi. Just one single example of this small tree was found growing on a scree slope on Three Kings Island (55 km northwest of Cape Reinga) in 1945. Careful cuttings were taken from this last survivor, in the hope of growing more specimens, and eventually one of its 'children' produced seeds. The kaikōmako grown from those seeds grew successfully and produced their own seeds, and the species has now been replanted on the islands and on the mainland too, in private and public gardens.

To prevent ground plants — such as vines — from taking hold and growing up their trunks, and possibly compromising growth, some trees, such as rimu and kauri, regularly shed the outer layers of their bark in large flakes. Many trees routinely shed their bark — new growth in the trunk gradually forces old bark to fall away in pieces to allow for the trunk's expansion.

Rātā

The title of premier native climber must go to the northern rātā, found throughout the North Island and upper parts of the South Island. It establishes itself much like the other climbing plants, gripping and growing encircling stems and roots on the host tree — such as miro, pukatea, Pūriri, rimu or kahikatea. Roots descend from the rātā as it grows higher and larger, and it eventually totally encompasses its supporting tree. The roots grow stronger and thicker and essentially become trunks in their own right. Now almost smothered, the host tree may eventually die and rot away, leaving the rātā standing entirely on its own, as an independent tree, perhaps up to 40m in height, and with a lifespan of up to 300 years. The rātā in bloom is a mass of red blossoms, very similar in nature to that of the pōhutukawa, its close relative. The nectar is drunk by kākā, kea, bellbirds and tūī. Unfortunately, the rātā's new growing leaves — and those of the pōhutukawa — are a favourite of possums, resulting in many trees being destroyed.

The rātā vine — rātāpiki — doesn't take over its host tree, but remains as a simple climber, with similar red blossoms. The small white rātā vine — akatea — is the same in habit, but bears white blossoms. The younger, slimmer vines of these two climbers had many uses for early Māori — especially lashings for buildings and tools.

Cicada — Kihikihi/Tātarakihi

When cicada nymphs living in the soils below the tree (see page 11) emerge after three or more years feeding on root tips, they climb up the tree trunk for a short distance and anchor themselves on the bark. In a short time, the hard outer skin splits, and the adult cicada wrestles its way out, leaving the hard empty case still attached to the trunk.

The adults live for about two months or more, and feed by sucking on tree sap. To find a mate, the male cicada announces his presence by drumming special body chambers, or by clapping wings against a hard surface. There are about 42 cicada species in New Zealand, and each makes its own distinctive sound. The largest and most common is the chorus cicada — kihikiki wawā. After mating, the female lays her eggs in the stem or branch of a tree, leaving a distinctive herringbone scar on the surface. After about two months, the young nymphs emerge from the eggs and drop to the ground, to find their way under the surface.

Bag Moth — Pū A Raukatauri

The homes of these moths — 6cm-long 'bags' — can often be seen hanging from the trunk outcrops and branches of many trees, especially kānuka, mānuka and macrocarpa. The bag, or case, is made from silk secreted by the caterpillar, and strengthened with tiny scraps and particles of vegetation, making it almost impossible to break or tear open. The caterpillar inside can move about at night — staying inside the bag — to munch on the leaves through a hole at the top of the bag. There's a hole at the bottom too, for droppings to fall out. When the adult moths have pupated, the female moth remains inside the bag in a grub-like state — lacking wings or legs — while males develop as 'proper' moths. The adults do not feed and live for only a few hours; just long enough for the flying male to find a mate. The Māori name refers to the flute of the goddess of music, Hine Raukatauri. The Māori flute — pūtōrino — is shaped like the bag moth's home.

There are about 50 species of bag moth in New Zealand, and 1350 known around the world.

North Island Lichen Moth

This moth's name is well deserved — when resting on tree lichens, with wings folded, it's almost impossible to see. The wing patterns serve a double purpose; while they blend with the lights and shades of the lichen, as a form of camouflage, the wing patterns are not symmetrical — that is, they don't exactly match each other, so predators may not see the expected 'giveaway' of mirror-image wings. The moth measures about 4–5cm with wings outspread.

The moth's caterpillars are well-disguised, too. Brown and blotchy-white, they resemble small twigs when standing erect on a branch, or bird droppings when lying flat, or curled on a leaf. They feed on lichen, and the leaves of the Five-finger tree — whaupaku/whauwhaupaku.

The South Island species of lichen moth is slightly larger, but with less patterning to its wings. It is also called the zebra lichen moth and appears on the reverse of New Zealand's $100 note.

Exquisite Carpet Moth

There are many species of moths that have lichen-patterned forewings, and the exquisite carpet moth is one of the prettiest. When at rest on lichen-covered tree trunks in South Island forests, it's almost impossible to make out — its green-grey markings are a perfect match with similarly-coloured lichens. Its open wingspan is about 30mm.

This moth and the North Island lichen moth both belong to a group of moths called looper moths — known as tāwhana to Māori. The name comes from the movement of their caterpillars — having legs at the front and rear, and none near the centre, they move by going forward with the rear legs, pushing the centre upwards into a loop, and then the front legs walk on until the caterpillar is straight and then the action is repeated. There are about 160,000 species known, and nearly 300 species in New Zealand. Our total population of moth species is around 1800.

Huhu Beetle — Tunga Rere

At 4–5cm long, this is the largest and heaviest of all our native beetles. It's usually found in dense bush and forests. The first three years of its life are spent as a large grub living inside old tree trunks and chewing on rotten wood. The term 'huhu' is generally used by Māori to refer to the grub only, not the adult beetle. The fat, 7cm-long grubs have long been a favourite food source of others — at least two other beetle larvae prey on them and the kiwi can probe rotted logs to extract the grubs. Māori would traditionally fry or roast the grubs, or just eat them raw. The adult beetle that eventually emerges lives only for a few weeks — just enough time to find a mate and lay eggs. The beetle doesn't eat during this time, but still has jaws strong enough to give a painful nip to an inquisitive predator or human finger. It's a blundering, clattering flyer, and often strays into houses, attracted by lights.

It's a member of the longhorn beetle family — named for the extra-long antennae that are even longer than their bodies. There are about 200 related species in New Zealand, including the kānuka longhorn beetle (below), and some 25,000 known around the world.

The largest pōhutukawa tree in New Zealand grows at Te Araroa, near East Cape. Named after a local chief, it's known as 'Te Waha o Rerekohu' (the mouth of Rerekohu). It has about 22 trunks, measuring over 20m in circumference. The tree has recently been found to be infected with myrtle rust, which is usually fatal for such trees. It's reckoned to be about 600 years old, and there is a pōhutukawa at Cape Reinga thought to be about 800 years old.

Kānuka Longhorn Beetle

Appearing as a slightly smaller and smoother version of its relative the huhu beetle, the larvae of the kānuka longhorn are often found tunnelling and feeding in kānuka and mānuka trees, as well as some beech trees. Their multiple tunnels can be up to a metre in length inside the tree's sapwood, with short horizontal passages to the surface. The grubs are very similar to the huhu, and birds such as kākā are able to dig them out of their tunnels. When ready to pupate, the grub creates a larger chamber with a 'door' made from roughly shredded wood. The new adult easily breaks through this and flies off. This vacant chamber is sometimes occupied by tree wētā.

Giant Centipede — Hura/Hara

Found mostly in the upper North Island forests and offshore islands, this 25cm-long giant rests in leaf litter and under logs by day and comes out at night to roam the ground and up and down trees and stumps to search out food. Its front legs are also poisonous pincer jaws, and it can catch and kill a great range of prey — from beetles and spiders to worms and even lizards. Its bite is not poisonous to humans but is extremely painful. The body is segmented, with one pair of legs to each segment. So that the centipede doesn't entangle its legs and trip itself up, each pair is slightly longer that the pair immediately in front. It's the largest of at least 35 centipede species in New Zealand, and there are about 8000 species around the world.

The world's tallest living tree is a giant redwood called Hyperion, in California, USA. It measures 116.07m in height. In the same national park are the second, fourth and fifth tallest trees known, at heights of 114.91m, 113.08m and 110.64m.

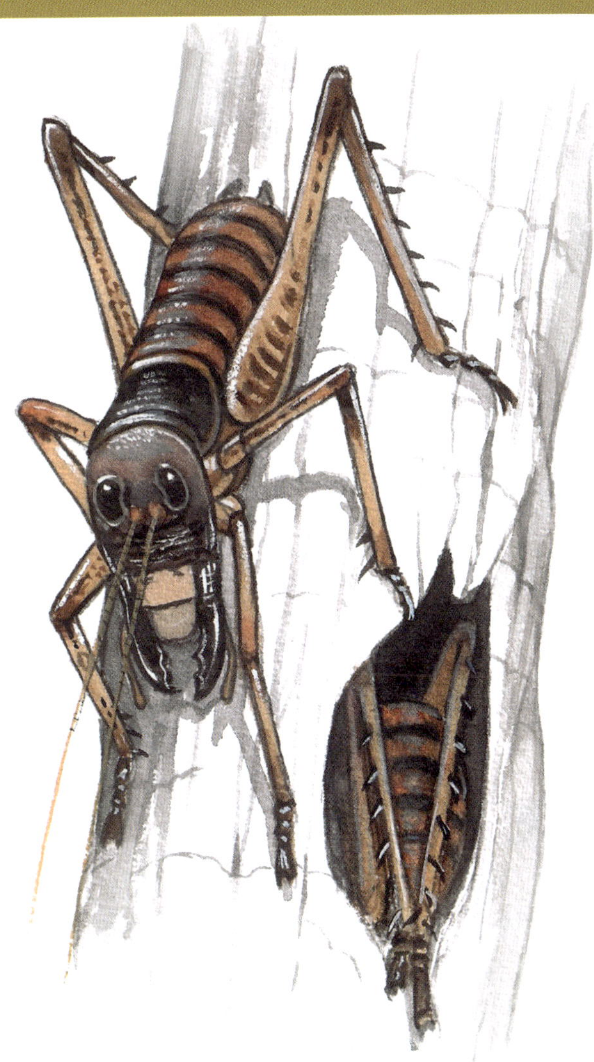

Tree Wētā — Pūtangatanga

Tree wētā take advantage of any crevice or hole in a tree trunk to make their home. They remain inside during the day — facing backwards, so their spiny legs present a fearsome barrier to any predator or intruder, such as rats or birds — or other wētā looking for a home. At night, they emerge to feed on insects and new plant leaves. If disturbed and handled carelessly, they can kick or scratch with their spiny legs, or give a painful bite with their strong jaws. The small discs below the knees of the front legs are actually its ears, and the long spike on the rear of some wētā is not a weapon, but the female's ovipositor, which she uses to lay her eggs in any available damp and secluded spot, such as rotten tree bark. There are 7 known species of tree wētā, with a body length of around 7cm, and they can live for 8 years or more.

Black Tunnelweb Spider

This spider creates a silk-lined home under logs, stones and in any crevice or hole it can find in tree trunks. The small holes, with their webbed surrounds are usually easy to see, especially in the trunks of ponga tree ferns. Inside, the spider waits for possible prey — beetles and slaters, for example — to touch the silk as it passes by. The spider detects the slight vibration in the silk and then rushes out to attack with strong downward-facing fangs. Though not venomous to humans, these spiders can still inflict painful bites.

They are robust spiders, with body lengths of nearly 3cm, and leg spans up to 5cm. There are about 25 spiders of this type in New Zealand, and the black tunnelweb spider is the strongest and the heaviest of all New Zealand spiders — it can even attack a garden snail, biting and holding on, so that the dying snail can't withdraw into its shell.

Although most spiders live only for 1–3 years, the tunnelweb spiders can live for 10 years or more.

White-tailed Spider

Rather than catch and eat the usual spider fare of insects such as beetles and flies, the white-tailed spider prefers to aggressively hunt other spiders. Even during mating, if a male spider attempts to approach a female without first getting a 'safe' signal from her, he will likely be eaten. These spiders live under stones, bark and leaf litter in bush and gardens, and roam mostly in the evening and at night to hunt out their prey.

One method it uses is to approach the outer 'webbing' of a hole-dwelling spider — such as that of the tunnelweb spider in trees, or the tangled web of the grey house spider under house weatherboards. (both spiders are more than twice the size of the 1.5cm-long white-tailed spider). It gently 'tickles' the silky strands in imitation of a passing insect, and when the resident spider rushes out, the white-tailed spider attacks.

This spider came from Australia in the late 1800s and can give quite a nasty bite to humans if disturbed. Over recent years, bites from white-tailed spiders have been suspected of causing necrotic ulcers — that is, a sore which is very slow to heal, or even spread through the skin — but this is yet to be actually proven.

Nīkau Moth

This pretty little moth — with just a 2cm wingspan — is common throughout North Island forests. It can be seen resting head downwards on the trunks of nīkau palm trees. Its caterpillars live on and in the nīkau's red berries and leaf bases. When they're ready to pupate, the grubs travel down to the trunk's ringed leaf scars to construct a pale oval cocoon with flattened ends.

Red Admiral Butterfly — Kahukura

While this butterfly takes nectar from many different flowers, such as those of the *Buddleia* plant (also known as the butterfly plant), its alternate food is the sap seepage that leaks from many trees, especially that from beech trees, and it's often seen resting on their trunks. It's more commonly seen from mid to late summer, and it's quite long-lived — often from 6 to 9 months. Some individuals can 'overwinter' in a state of mild hibernation, and become active on warmer, milder winter days.

The red admiral mostly lays its eggs on the tree nettle — ongaonga — where the emerging caterpillars are mostly protected by casual predators by the sharp toxic needles. For further protection, the caterpillars pull over the leaf tips and use their silk to secure them to construct 'tents' in which to live and feed. There are more than 25 butterfly species in New Zealand, and about 17,500 known around the world.

The Māori name means 'red cloak'.

Pūriri Moth

With a wingspan of up to 15cm, this is the largest of all New Zealand's flying insects. It has greatly variable wing markings and patterns, appearing in a range of greens, browns and yellows. The adult moth lives only for 1–3 days — just long enough for a mate to be found, and then for the female to lay her fertilised eggs — up to 2000 — on the forest floor. The moths have no mouth parts, and therefore don't eat during their short adult life. Being so large and relatively slow and clumsy when on the ground, they are often prey for rats and cats, and can be taken by bats and moreporks (ruru) when in flight.

After hatching, the tiny caterpillars live for about a year eating fungi under decaying wood, before climbing a nearby tree — sometimes beech, tītoki, houhere, kānuka or makomako, but especially pūriri.

Here, they can live in tunnels where they eat away at the sapwood and inner bark for up to 6 years or more, and growing fat and big enough to earn the title of our largest native grub — up to 12cm in length. When the grub pupates, and leaves the tunnels as an adult, tree wētā sometimes take up the vacancy.

Elephant Weevil

It's plain how this 2cm-long insect gets its name — from its long proboscis, or snout. Although it's a capable flyer, it generally prefers to roam around the trunks of kauri, beech, rimu and taraire trees, to feed on sap. The weevil grubs feed on all sorts of plant material, including fruit, stems, roots, fungi and live or rotten wood. They often tunnel into the decaying branches or trunks of these trees, but they're not safe from predators — the giant ichneumonoid wasp has an extraordinarily long ovipositor (egg-laying spike) with which it can drill through the wood and lay eggs in the now-paralysed grub's body. When the wasp eggs hatch, they have a ready meal waiting.

Giraffe Weevil — Tūwhaipapa

Our longest beetle — up to 9cm long. While the male weevil has long antennae at the very end of its rostrum, or snout, the smaller female's are set much further back, to allow her to chew and bore into a tree's dead wood to lay her eggs. The resulting grubs live in tunnels in the wood for about two years before emerging as adults, and through a hole opening that's actually square, rather than round. They can live for about 2–3 weeks, and despite their unlikely appearance, these weevils can fly. They rest in the tree's canopy at night, then roam the tree in the daytime, to feed on sap. If disturbed, they will fall from the tree into the leaf litter below, and 'play dead' for up to an hour.

Giraffe weevils sometimes congregate in large numbers — up to 60 have been found on just a single tree. The males occasionally do battle, when competing for the attentions of a female — they can bite with the tiny mandibles at the end of the long rostrum, or simply use it as a weapon, and sometimes younger and smaller males will sneak in to mate unnoticed, while the fights continue.

They're found in the forests of the North Island and in the upper South Island, usually on native trees such as karaka, mahoe, rimu and rewarewa.

Both Māori and later European settlers found many uses for the timber from our native trees. Besides the obvious end results of housing, fencing, tools and weapons for Māori settlers, and countless new applications that new European settlers required — wheels, wharves, buildings, furniture, barrels and so on — it's kauri and tōtara that are the most useful.

While they both are widely used to construct buildings, early Māori prized them most highly for their suitability to building waka. A full-sized war canoe — waka toa — can be carved from a single felled tōtara trunk. Tōtara is usually the timber of choice for the large carvings adorning a marae's wharenui, too.

Rifleman — Tītīpounamu

This little bird — New Zealand's smallest at just 8cm long from bill-tip to tail-end and weighing no more than 6–7g — gets its English name from European settlers, who were reminded of the green-jacketed rifle regiments. And Māori named it for its similarity to greenstone — pounamu.

It's found in most South Island forests, especially beech, and in some locations in the North Island, including kauri and kamahi forests. It's something of a reluctant flyer, usually only taking to the air for a practical reason, such as moving to a neighbouring tree. It nests in tree holes, and forages for flies, small grubs, beetles and spiders on the tree's branches and trunk. It has an unusual method for feeding — it climbs and hops upwards around the trunk, circling as though climbing a spiral staircase as it picks and pokes at the crevices in the tree's bark, for its small prey.

The rifleman generally lives for about 6 years.

Veined Slug — Putoko Ropiropi

There are at least 30 species of native veined slugs. They get their name from the leaf-like pattern on their bodies. Most are found in bush and forest, where they come out to graze in the evenings through leaf litter and up into tree and shrub leaves for fungi, algae and lichen. They can be anywhere between 5–15cm in length, with smooth or bumpy surfaces, and appear in a wide variety of colours — orange, brown, yellow, cream — and the green-coloured species have the best camouflage of all, with their colour and vein pattern often matching the leaf they're on. The breathing hole — difficult to discern with garden slugs — is much more obvious on the bodies of veined slugs. These natives only have a single pair of tentacles, unlike the introduced species, which have two pairs.

Veined slugs often gather in groups when there's a good source of food.

Kauri Snail — Pūpū Rangi

Not named because it lives exclusively around kauri trees, but for the fact that it's found in the Far North's kauri forests. Living for 20 years or more, this carnivorous snail hunts through the damp leaf litter on the forest floor for small animals such as insects and their larvae, slugs and earthworms — a favourite food — and even for other, smaller, kauri snails. They actually avoid foraging around kauri trees as the nearby ground is usually too dry for worms. It has a very strong muscular foot and can climb tree trunks for some distance. After mating, which can take up to 10 hours, the snail lays 10–12 white eggs — about 1cm long — in mounds of rotten leaves on the forest floor. The resulting juveniles can spend part of their growing period living in trees for protection — up to 6 metres or more above the ground.

Once more widespread in our forests, these and other giant snail species have fallen prey to introduced animals such as rats, possums and pigs, and have also suffered from habitat destruction.

IN AND OUT OF THE BRANCHES

Up at the top of the tree is the canopy — where the trunk eventually separates into branches sent in all directions to hold out the leaves that drive the top end of the tree's requirement for food and energy — deriving sugars from sunlight through the process of photosynthesis.

It also presents a complicated and interconnected maze of places and opportunities for other life to exploit — for food, protection, accommodation and predation. The canopy environment and its attendant community in a single mature tree can be one of the most varied and complex to be seen . . . it's an entirely separate and unique ecosystem.

Perching Lily — Kahakaha

Many plants find a home nestled in the branches of trees. One of the most substantial is the perching lily. It can grow and reproduce to such an extent that the plants may even form their own extensive 'garden' high in the tree. Some become so heavy that they break one of the supporting branches and crash to the ground — earning them the name of 'widowmakers' from early Europeans, due to the danger they presented. The lily's leaves were used by Māori for weaving sandals and for making baskets in which to cook eel and other foods. The red berries are also edible, enjoyed by humans, tūī and kererū, and the nectar of the 30cm flower spikes is a favourite with bats.

As the lily can't derive water from the ground, its leaves have become V-shaped, in order to bring rainwater to its small root system. The water pooled at the base of 1.5m leaves is the exclusive breeding home of one of our native mosquito species.

Old Man's Beard Lichen — Angiangi

This wispy grey-green fruticose lichen can be seen hanging from the branches of many forest trees, but especially beech and pine. The wind-blown spores are caught in branches, and they will take and grow if the tree is suitable. Angiangi translates as 'lungs of the forest' as the lichen seems to do best where there is reasonable movement of fresh air. Māori have long known that this lichen has several antibacterial, antiseptic and antibiotic properties, and preparations of it have many medicinal uses, including treating certain infections and ailments. It's also useful in stemming blood flow and treating wounds. This lichen can grow for many years and reaches lengths of 20cm or more. There are about 28 related beard lichen species in New Zealand, and they shouldn't be confused with the pest vine called 'old man's beard' (page 17).

Red Mistletoe — Pikirangi/Pirinoa

This pretty mistletoe is common throughout beech forests in both the North and South Islands, and can also make its home high in towai, pūriri and pōhutukawa trees. It can grow into a large shrub over a metre in height. There are 8 species of native mistletoe — two bear great masses of red flowers, and the rest have green, yellow or white flowers. The tight flowers need to be twisted open — usually by birds such as bellbirds and tūī seeking the nectar inside — and the petals then spring apart and coat the bird with pollen, which they then carry to other flowers, and complete the necessary fertilisation. The mistletoe can then produce its bright red berries, which are eaten by many birds who then pass the seeds as they visit and settle on other trees. Early Māori children made a sort of pleasant chewing-gum from the pulped red berries.

Native mistletoes are partly parasitic, which means that while they bear leaves for photosynthesis, they also send roots into the host tree to take water and more nutrients.

In places, this plant is under threat from browsing by possums, insect damage and loss of forest habitat.

Easter Orchid — Raupeka

Orchids are one of the greatest families of flowering plants. There are about 28,000 species around the world, and about 80 species in New Zealand, found in all situations, from alpine to sea level, on the ground, growing on rocks or high in the branches of tall trees.

The easter orchid can be seen in most of our forests and its white flowers — about 8mm across — are some of the most strongly scented of all our native plants and can be easily sensed by trampers walking far below.

It seems that no epiphyte has exclusivity to a tree — there are always a great range of large and small plants living on the host. A survey of a single kauri tree in 1993 found that there were at least 36 different plants growing in its branches.

Drooping Spleenwort — Ngā Makawe O Raukatauri

This epiphytic fern can be found in many forests around the country, including: beech, kauri, podocarp forest (e.g. rimu, miro and tōtara) and broadleaved forest (e.g. māhoe, taraire and tawa). It's also common in Australia and around the Pacific, and found in a variety of locations and environments, from shore to near alpine — and growing on the ground, in soil, on rocks or high up in a tree's crown. The Māori name translates as 'ringlets of the hair of the goddess of music.'

The spleenwort is typical of many fern species that take hold in the crowns of trees, as the result of wind-borne spores finding a home in the accumulated detritus where branches part — even some true ground ferns, like the hound's tongue fern — kowhaowhao — can find accommodation up there.

Honeydew

Honeydew is produced by tiny scale insects — essentially lacking legs or wings — living on and within the foliage and bark of the branches and trunks of many trees. Those living on beech trees take the sugary sap from the tree's phloem (the living inner bark), but as they take in far more than they actually need, they excrete the excess through a long anal tube, which looks like a very fine filament sticking out from the bark. This sticky sweet substance drips down and wets the leaves, branches and trunk. These tasty droplets are eagerly sought by birds such as bellbirds, kākā and tūi, who have even been seen to work their way around a tree, taking a drop from the end of each scale insect's anal tube as they go.

Plenty of others are keen on the sugary drops, too — bats, geckos, bees and other insects — even rats and possums have been known to take a few sips. Introduced wasps are a bit too keen, though. They have found that they can get extra sugary liquid by biting off the end of the scale insect's anal tube — and too many bites reduce the tube to the point where the scale insect dies. This has led to a 90% reduction of honeydew production in some places and has obviously removed a good source of food for all those other feeders.

The scale insect's close relative, the much larger aphid (see opposite), also produces honeydew, when sucking on the saps in wood, leaves and leaf stems. Ants will regularly 'milk' aphids for their honeydew by stroking their abdomens to encourage them to produce a drop or two of the sugary liquid. Some ants actually 'herd' and protect the aphids from predators — and some even take them home to the ant nest.

As the honeydew from the scale insects and aphids drips down and wets the tree, often a black sooty mould will appear and grow into a thick spongy mat. It appears mostly in beech, mānuka and kānuka forests. This mould in turn provides a form of food for others, including small beetles and moths. The mould does no harm to the tree, unless it forms on honeydew that has soaked leaves — reducing their capacity for photosynthesis. Too many leaves 'blanked out' this way can affect the tree's growth and health.

For centuries, Māori have used the leaves of many of our native trees for an incredible range of uses. Long leaves, such as those of the cabbage tree — tī kōuka — could be used for bird snares, capes, sandals, rope, mats and roof thatching. Similar uses could be found for the leaves of flax and the climbing kiekie (see page 16), which are also employed in creating tukutuku panels.

The long leafy fronds of the nīkau palm tree and those of the larger tree ferns were used for wall and roof thatching.

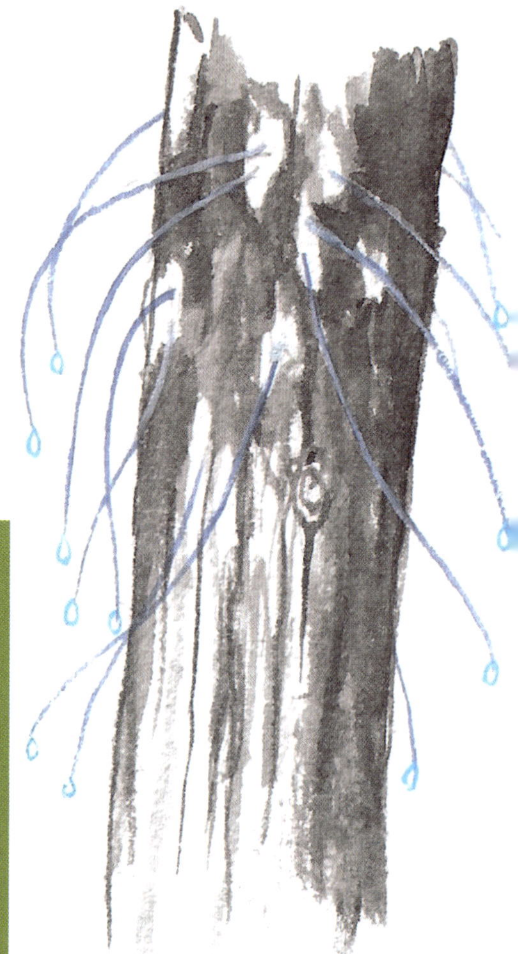

Tree sap, or gum, is the fluid used by trees to convey nutrients to growing parts and to maintain health — much like the blood system in animals. Many societies around the world harvest and process the sap from different tree species for a variety of purposes — for medicinal and laboratory purposes, waterproofing, and for foodstuffs, such as maple syrup. The gum from our own kauri trees was once much sought after and was valued in its use in making varnishes and paint. For a period in the late 1800s, kauri gum exports were worth more than those of gold. Māori used the gum from kauri and other trees such as tarata for burning torches at night, for making dyes from its soot, and even used it as a form of chewing gum.

Aphids — Kuturiki

These small insects, no more than 2–3mm in length, use a proboscis — a needle-like part of their mouths — to pierce growing leaf and plant stems to take up the sweet sap, and then excrete the excess as honeydew. While the aphids and their honeydew can be a benefit in bush and forest, just like the scale insects, they can be more of a problem on garden plants and on fruit trees.

There are nearly 100 different species in New Zealand — about 2250 species around the world — in a wide range of colours, and many have their own individual preference for the tree or plant that they live on. A recent aphid newcomer to New Zealand is the giant willow aphid, about twice the size of our native aphids. It lives almost exclusively on willow trees. Most aphids live for about a month.

They can appear in great numbers — it's reckoned that the aphid population of just one hectare of vegetation can produce 2 tonnes of honeydew in a single day! While many animals seek out the aphid's tasty honeydew, others are more interested in eating the aphids themselves, and they make a tasty snack for birds, ladybirds, wasps and praying mantises.

Ladybirds — Mumutawa

There are about 5000 ladybird species known around the world, and New Zealand has 40 species of these small — 7–10mm — beetles. About half of them have been introduced here to help to control insect pests. The eleven-spotted ladybird was possibly the first animal brought here for that purpose, in 1874. The steelblue ladybird was introduced from Australia to control scale insects on citrus plants.

They are natural predators of scale insects, aphids and mites, and a single ladybird can consume up to 100 aphids per day. During its one-year lifespan, an adult ladybird can eat around 5000 aphids. They will find aphids and scale insects wherever they may be — high on forest tree branches, such as rimu and beech, on fruit trees, flax plants and on garden and vegetable plants. Often, a ladybird will lay her eggs close to aphid colonies, so that her young will have a ready meal waiting when they hatch — and those young grubs can manage to eat 50 aphids a day.

Honeybee — Pī Honi

Now common throughout New Zealand, honeybees were first introduced here from Australia in 1839, and released around the Hokianga, for the purpose of plant pollination, and to begin a trade in 'farmed' honey. Although there are plenty of native bees, they were generally found to be too small to pollinate the flowers of the newly introduced crops.

Besides those bees foraging from manufactured artificial beehives, there are many more colonies living out in the wild. Here, they build hives in the crooks of tree branches, in cavities in tree trunks, rocks and buildings. There can be up to 60,000 worker bees in a hive, with hundreds of male drones and just a single queen bee. She can lay 2000–3000 eggs every day, and these are cared for by the worker bees.

A single bee can visit perhaps 1000 flowers in a single day — gathering nectar to make honey and collecting pollen to store in little bags on their back legs. Back at the hive, workers produce beeswax from special glands to build the many cells of the honeycomb. These cells house the larvae that hatch from the queen's eggs, and also store pollen nectar and honey.

When a good source of pollen and nectar has been found, the bee will return to the hive to perform a special dance, which tells the other bees where to go, how far it is and even how much pollen and nectar there is.

Stick Insects — Rō/Whē

There are 16 species of flightless stick insects in New Zealand, and they appear in a wide range of sizes and colours — from very smooth to rough or even covered in short spines, and may be coloured green, brown, grey or mottled in black and white. They usually live for about a year. Size can range from 5–15cm in length. The male is usually much smaller than the female, and in at least one species no males have ever been seen — the female just produces female eggs and young.

Stick insects are mostly inactive during the day, resting on branches with front legs stretched out straight, so that the whole insect looks like a twig or stem. They roam about at night feeding on leaves, most commonly those of pōhutukawa, mānuka and kānuka trees. One rough brown species prefers the leaves of the bush lawyer vine (page 18). When a stick insect is on the move, it has a very wobbly, wavering way of walking, and if disturbed will often just 'freeze' in the sleep position. Some species will stiffen and fall to the ground like a twig and remain motionless for a while.

If caught by a bird or other predator, the stick insect can detach a leg in order to escape. Young stick insects can even regrow the missing limb.

Leafminer Moths

Lines and marks on a tree's leaves are often a sign that the tiny caterpillars of leafminer moths are at work inside. Some lines appear as random squiggles, as the tiny caterpillars just chew their way haphazardly through the leaf's insides. Some caterpillars are more consistent — moving backwards and forwards, up and down, to leave regular swirls visible, or zig-zag tracks. Often the fine see-through outer surface of the leaf is left intact.

Different leafminer moth species have their own tree preferences — kauri, beech, wattle and lancewood, for example, all have their own particular leaf-eaters.

There are about 60 leafminer moth species in New Zealand.

Cabbage Tree Moth

This moth has an almost perfect disguise when at rest on the old or dead leaves of cabbage trees. Here, the straight-line patterns on its pale grey-brown wings — pressed flat against the leaf, so as to leave no telltale shadow to predators — are aligned with the lines of the veins on the leaf. It has a wingspan of about 6cm and its small green caterpillars live down in the bases of the leaves and emerge at night to chew on them, leaving notches and holes. This moth is another member of the looper moth group (page 21).

Gum Emperor Moth

This large, furry moth — with a wingspan up to 10cm — was accidentally introduced from Australia to Whanganui in 1915 and has now spread throughout the North Island and the upper South Island. It prefers to live around silver birch, gum trees and pepper trees. When caterpillars emerge from eggs laid in summer, they eat the leaves of the host tree until they grow large enough to spin a large, silk-hairy cocoon — taking about 10 hours to complete. The bright green caterpillar can reach 12cm in length. Inside the cocoon, the caterpillar hibernates through winter before breaking free as the adult moth.

The 'eyes' on the moth's wings help to startle possible predators, such as birds, when the wings are opened and closed repeatedly.

There are two similar species in New Zealand, and about 1200 known around the world.

Lemon Tree Borer

The 1.5cm long lemon tree borer is a member of the same beetle family as the huhu and kānuka longhorn beetles. They're found around the North Island and the upper South Island. After the adult beetle lays eggs, the grubs make a network of tunnels in the branches of citrus trees and forest trees such as rangiora and māhoe. They live and grow in their tunnels for about 18–20 months or more, and the adult may live for about two more months. If disturbed by predators, the beetle can emit a 'squeak' by rubbing against the ridged area behind its head. They hide during the day and venture out at night to feed on nectar and pollen.

There are nearly 200 species of longhorn beetles in New Zealand, and each has its own preference for the plants and trees they choose to call home, including beech, tawa, kōwhai, tāwari, rimu, kahikatea, mānuka, karaka and even mangrove.

Early Māori employed many tree leaf preparations for a wide variety of personal uses, including Pūriri leaves to treat wounds, ulcers and sore throats, and kohekohe leaves as an antidote to poisonings. Ngaio leaves rubbed onto the skin serve as a good insect repellent and chewing koromiko leaves helped ease constipation and diarrhoea. A form of tea can be made from the peppery leaves of kawakawa, and crushed tarata leaves provide a pleasant lemony scent for hair and body.

Flower Longhorn Beetle

This very distinctive and tiny flying beetle — just 5–7mm long — is found throughout the country. It's an important pollinator, as it feeds on the pollen and nectar from the blossoms of a great range of trees and smaller plants. It's common to see the beetles in considerable numbers around the flowers of garden and orchard plants (such as avocado and kiwifruit), harakeke (flax), and the flowers of trees such as red beech, silver beech, kaikōmako, matagouri and others. These beetles mate and feed on the flowers they visit, and the males often fight with each other, even when there are no females present. After mating, the female flies off to lay her eggs under tree bark or in broken or dead branches. There are 10 species of flower longhorn beetles in New Zealand.

Mānuka Chafer Beetle — Kēkerewai

These beetles range in size from 3–20mm in length, and although most are green, they can be found in a range of colours, including orange, brown, red, purple or even blue. Larvae and beetles favour mānuka trees. The eggs are laid in the nearby soil, and, when hatched, the larvae feed on the mānuka's roots for almost two years before emerging as adults. The beetles climb the mānuka's trunk — often in great numbers — to feed on the foliage. It's been found that the oils in the mānuka's leaves actually help to strengthen the beetles' elytra (wing cases).

Any decent wind will cause beetles to fall from the trees, and when close to water, fish — especially trout — will eagerly scoop them up. Beetles on the ground also make ready snacks for foraging mice and sparrows. Early Māori collected the fallen beetles for food — sometimes cooked with pollen from raupō plants. Antiseptic properties in the beetle also aided the reduction of stomach aches and fevers.

Praying Mantis — Rō/Whē

The 4cm-long praying mantis waits patiently on leaves, with its long, spiny front legs tucked together in a 'prayerful' pose, then, when possible prey comes within range — usually beetles, cicadas, moths or flies — it lunges out in a flash to grab the victim. A single mantis can consume well over 20 captives in a day.

This insect has very good eyesight and will turn and follow any inquisitive finger with its eyes. They can be found throughout New Zealand.

Since the 1970s, the African praying mantis has spread through the upper North Island. It's very similar in appearance, but has green and brown colouring, rather than the plain green of the New Zealand species, and it lacks the purple and blue patch on the inside of its front legs. It prefers to wait for prey on the underside of leaves, while the New Zealand mantis stays on top.

The New Zealand female lays her eggs in a neat zipper-like case, but the African egg case is a rougher, foamy-looking affair. Both can be seen attached to any hard surface, such as tree trunks, posts and houses. When they hatch, the young appear as tiny miniatures of the adult insect.

The loneliest tree in the world might be an Acacia tree known as the Tree of Life, standing in the desert in Bahrain — almost nothing but sand to be seen in all directions. It's nearly 10m in height and is about 400 years old. It's unclear how the tree has managed to thrive and maintain healthy foliage, as Bahrain has almost no rain throughout the year. Its roots have been determined to be about 50m deep, so perhaps there's sufficient moisture at that depth to enable it to survive. It's visited by about 65,000 people a year, and even has its own visitor centre.

Common Blue Butterfly — Pepe Ao Ruri

In summertime, these little butterflies — wingspan of about 2.5cm — can be seen flying close to the ground in gardens, pastures and farmlands in lowlands and in higher country. They also frequent riverbanks, seashores and estuaries, and here they're attracted to the flowers on mangrove trees. Mostly blue-purple or grey-blue above, the wings are silvery-grey underneath. The wings become greyer with age.

On very bright days, they rest on rocks, plants or grass with their wings closed, but on cooler or cloudier days they'll rest with wings slightly open, facing away from the sun. If approached, they take to the air in a jerky fluttering-stuttering flight, which can make it hard for any possible predator to follow. They're very common through the North Island and in the north and west of the South Island.

Eggs are laid individually on the stems and under the leaves of a range of small food plants, including clover, lucerne and broom, and the resulting little green caterpillars can sometimes be in numbers sufficient to be considered a crop pest in some places. The adult butterflies usually live for just a few days, although some females can live for a couple of weeks.

Giant Wētā

There are 11 species of giant wētā — our largest and heaviest insect. They can regularly reach up to 10cm in body length and weigh around 35g. The largest species of all is the Little Barrier Island giant wētā — wētāpunga — and one individual was once recorded with a weight of 71g — that's about the weight of a song thrush or a pair of sparrows!

Some giant wētā species are found in alpine regions, where they are ground-dwelling, but those species in protected reserves and offshore islands around the north of the North Island are more adventurous. During the day, they hide under the long, hanging fronds of tree ferns and cabbage tree leaves, under loose bark or in tree cavities, with their long spiny legs tucked in tightly for protection. In the evening, they climb up to eat the new leaves of smaller trees such as karaka, māhoe and kohekohe. They will also eat small insects, fruit and some fungi.

Most giant wētā take up to 2 years to reach their full adult size, with a total lifespan of perhaps 3–4 years.

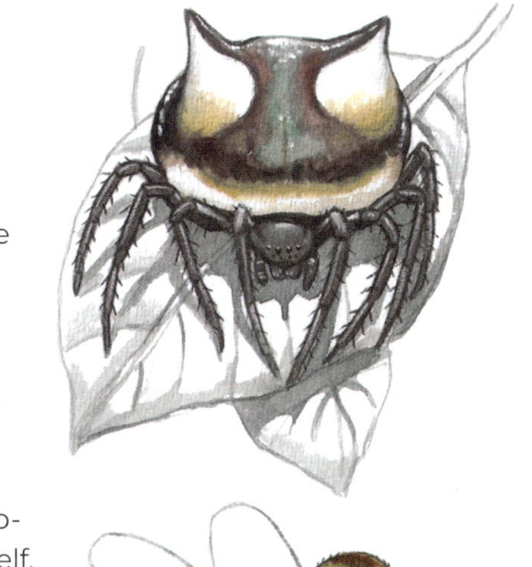

Two-Spined Spider

Measuring less than 1cm across the body, these little Australian spiders have been found in New Zealand since the 1970s and are now quite common in much of the North Island and have also been recorded in the Nelson and Christchurch regions. Only the female has the distinctive shape and colouring — the male is less than half her size and is a dull, mottled brown. For obvious reasons, these spiders belong to a group known as 'bird-dropping spiders'.

Unusually for spiders, the female can alter her colouring if disturbed, by sending colour 'pulses' through the yellow and cream bands. She spends her days hiding under leaves, and then comes out at night to build a cartwheel-shaped web, to trap moths and other insects. The two-spined spider is strong enough to capture insects much bigger than itself.

At dawn, she eats up her web, and withdraws to her hiding place. Her spindle-shaped brown paper-like egg case — almost twice her size — can be found under nearby leaves.

Nursery Web Spider

This spider's webs can be seen covering the tops of gorse and other shrubby plants, and also on the ends of the branches of mānuka. The webs are not built to catch prey but are literally nurseries for the spider's young. After carrying a large egg sac around with her for a month or more, when her eggs begin to hatch, she attaches the sac to the topmost leaves and builds the protective web — up to 15cm across — around it. She guards the nursery web until her young spiderlings — up to 200 of them — are ready to crawl out. Shortly afterwards they each let out a fine silken thread which is caught by the wind and lifts them away — this is called 'ballooning'.

Nursery web spiders catch prey — such as insects, small earthworms, bees and other spiders — by ambush or 'on the run'. They can be greedy too, grabbing new prey while already holding previous captives, and while still eating earlier ones. They roam mostly at night, around trees, shrubs, on the ground and around the stones at the edge of water courses. They're substantial spiders — up to 2cm in body length — with a leg span of 6cm or more.

Flower Spider

These very tiny spiders — with a body length of only around 3–6mm — are members of a group called crab spiders. They don't build webs but instead wait motionless on the leaves and flowers of shrubs and trees with their extra-long 2 front pairs of legs held out wide like a crab — ready to pounce on any small insect that comes close while visiting the flower. And just like crabs, they can scuttle sideways if threatened, running off and under the flower or leaf to hide.

They appear in a wide range of colours — greens, yellows, browns, reds — matching their chosen haunts, and some can alter their colourings to suit. The female often places her egg sac between leaves or blades of grass and protects it by tying the leaves together with silk. When they hatch, she feeds the young spiderlings with the small insects she catches, but if the food runs out, sometimes she gets eaten instead.

Shore Skink — Moko/ Mokomoko

The shore skink stays close to the north-eastern coasts of the North Island, roaming dunes and clumps of seaweeds and driftwood to seek out insects and spiders. But one of its favourite foods is the melon-flavoured and slightly peppery fruit of the pepper tree — kawakawa. It can climb several metres up to the very top of the tree, where the fruit spikes first appear in summer. Sometimes, the skink will break off the finger-length fruit spike and fall back to the ground with it. This small skink — body length of around 8cm not including the tail — can appear in a range of colours, depending on the nature of its chosen habitat; it may be in shades and patterns of brown, grey, green or even almost entirely black. It can live for about 10 years.

Nearly all skink species spend most of their lives on or close to the ground, scurrying through leaf litter and low vegetation, around rocks and under fallen logs. But they are all good climbers and will venture up tree trunks as they forage for prey, and further up again for any low-hanging berries and fruit. Some species — such as the striped skink — have been found to make their homes around kiekie and other epiphytes on trees. They are cold-blooded, which means that they need to bask motionless in the sun for a while to become properly active. But if disturbed, a skink can shed its tail as a twitching decoy while it escapes. The tail will later regrow, but probably smaller than the original. There are 78 skink species so far described in New Zealand.

It's not just birds and insects that enjoy the fruits borne on our trees, but humans too. Early Māori made cakes and puddings from the berries of hīnau, makomako and kōtukutuku, for example. The hard kernels of the fruits of tawa and karaka were often roasted and steamed and kept in storehouses for years before being cooked to eat. The tiny berries of tōtara and kahikatea were harvested in great numbers to add to food, and a form of jam could be made from makomako berries. Even the small fruit spikes of kawakawa could be used as flavourings. While the fruits of the tītoki are not especially sweet, early Māori found that an excellent hair oil could be obtained from its black seeds. And while the fruits of puka were pleasant to eat, they could also be used to make a glue, and often used to attach feathers to tools and weapons.

Elegant Gecko — Moko Kākāriki

The elegant gecko is common in forests in the central and northern North Island. Like many gecko species, it spends nearly all its life living in and roaming through the branches and foliage of trees during daylight. Mānuka/kānuka forest are a preference with many species. Their favourite foods are beetles, flies, moths, spiders and grubs, plus the trees' berries, fruit and the nectar from its flowers. This gecko will even take sips of scale insects' honeydew (page 30) when it's available. It measures up to 7cm in body length, not including the tail, and it can live for about 15 years or more. While its base colour is green, it can be plain or variously patterned with pale green, yellow or white outlined patches or long bars. Like skinks, geckos need to bask or 'sunbathe' to warm themselves sufficiently to be fully active, and so will usually go to the top or outermost branches to get the best sun exposure.

There are around 50 species of gecko in New Zealand and, as with skinks, new species are being discovered and described regularly. Many species have very restricted habitats — from small pockets of coast or forest to near-inaccessible scree slopes in alpine regions.

The Māori name for this gecko is also applied to other species of green gecko found in the Far North, the Wellington region, and in the South Island.

Forest Gecko — Moko pirirākau

Unlike the elegant gecko, this species — like most brown/grey geckos — is mostly active at night. It still likes to sunbathe and can be seen basking on tree branches and trunks, where its bark-like patterning makes for good camouflage. The colouring and patterns are quite variable — the brown/grey geckos can change these at will — with patches and spots that may be brown, grey, orange, red, yellow or green. Its body length is about 9cm, plus a tail that is longer than the body. It feeds on fruit, nectar, insects and spiders — sometimes waiting motionless for potential prey to walk by, rather than actively hunting for it. It can live for about 20 years.

The forest gecko is found in the upper North Island, Westland and Marlborough in the South Island, and very similar species can be found in the Wellington-Manawatu regions and other areas.

The honour of being the world's smallest tree goes to the dwarf willow tree. Just like its much larger relatives, it has a woody trunk, with true spreading branches . . . and it's barely 6cm tall! Some experts argue that it doesn't really qualify for the title, but there's no denying that it's a willow tree — it's just a very, very small one. It's a hardy plant, which has adapted to colder climates in the northern hemisphere and can found from sea level up to altitudes of 1500m.

Fantail — Pīwakawaka

One of New Zealand's most common birds — seen around trees in gardens, parks and forests throughout the country — the fantail will even accompany people on bush walks, eager to pick out any flying insects that the trampers may disturb. It very rarely feeds on the ground; instead, it catches insects in flight — flies, moths and beetles. Using its fanned tail (half the bird's 16cm length), it can practically stop-start in an instant and switch the direction of its stuttering flight as it chases prey through the air. The fantail will also hover along branches for a few seconds to pick off insects and spiders and will even flip upside down to get at prey hiding under leaves.

Their nests are usually built in the lower forks of trees, especially mānuka and kānuka. They are small and cup-shaped, and made from rotted wood fibres, mosses and dried grasses, all bound together with spiders' cobwebs.

Fantails weigh around 8g and can live for about 3 years. All-black fantails can be occasionally seen in the Wellington region and in the South Island.

The oldest tree in the world is a Great Basin bristlecone pine named Methuselah, growing in the White Mountains of California. It's estimated to be at least 4850 years old. Our own Tāne Mahuta — the largest living kauri — is about 2000–2500 years old. A previous giant kauri — Kairaru — was thought to be around 4000 years old when destroyed by a forest fire in the 1800s.

Blackbird — Manu Pango

Just edging out the starling — tāringi — and the house sparrow — tiu — for the title of New Zealand's most common bird, the blackbird was introduced here from Europe in the 1860s, and is now at home in parks, gardens and forests throughout the country. It's mostly a ground feeder — scratching at the ground or flicking the leaf litter with its bill to find insects, worms or small skinks — but it will also search branches for insects, seeds and berries. It has a habit of sometimes 'sunbathing' by resting on the ground with wings spread out. Nests are usually made of grasses and fine leaves held together by mud, and are set in small trees, low hedges or vegetation. Similar in size to the tūī, blackbirds can live for about 20 years.

Many introduced birds — house sparrow, song thrush, chaffinch (pahirini), starling, greenfinch, goldfinch, redpoll, myna, yellowhammer and so on — have similar habits; nesting low down in trees and shrubs and feeding mostly on the ground. Some will readily nest in tree holes, under shop verandas, house eaves, in roof gutters or in any available vacant space.

The 20m-tall umbrella-shaped Dragon Tree on the island of Tenerife, Spain has a trunk circumference of about 20m, and has a 6m-high internal cavity, which can be entered through a door fixed on the trunk. It boasts over 300 main branches, with 1800 smaller flowering branches. When the tree bears fruit, it's estimated that its weight increases by 3.5 tonnes.

Tūī

Except for areas of Otago and Canterbury, tūī can be seen throughout the country's gardens, parks and forests. They have a long brush-tipped tongue, which makes it easier for them to drink nectar from flowers. Favoured sources are the flowers of kowhai, rewarewa, rātā, pōhutukawa, Pūriri, kahikatea and flax. They are important pollinators, as they nearly always get a good covering of pollen as they thrust their bills deep into the flower. They'll also eat insects and the fruits of some trees.

Tūī are renowned for their song — a range of chuckles, coughs, twangs, bangs and whistles, with lots of sweet notes and trills. They can also imitate other birds' calls, and several devices such as car alarms and phone ringtones.

The tūī is a substantial bird, about 30cm long and weighing up to 120g and its lifespan is around 12 years.

Bellbird — Korimako

The smaller bellbird — korimako — is another brush-tongued bird, and is common through central and southern North Island forests, and the west coasts of the South Island. It, too, is an excellent singer, though its song is pretty and bell-like, and lacking the grunts and chuckles favoured by tūī. It likes the same nectars and food as the tūī, but the male will often chase off the female from the flowers, so her diet is mostly fruits, insects and spiders.

Bellbirds can live for about 8 years.

Stitchbird — Hihi

The third of our native brush-tipped tongue species is the small stitchbird — hihi — which is now restricted to offshore islands. Rather than build nests as the tūī and bellbird do, it usually nests in old tree holes. The bird's call of 't-zee' sounded like 'stitch' to early Europeans, while to Māori it was more like 'hi-hi'. They can live for about 7 years.

The leaves of rangiora are the largest of our native trees. They can measure up to 25cm long and 20cm wide. They are green on top and covered in fine white hairs underneath. While early Māori found that the leaves made a good poultice to treat inflammations and wounds, early European settlers also found the leaves to be a good substitute for toilet paper — calling the plant 'bushman's friend'.

Grey Warbler — Riroriro

This 11cm-long bird has a sweet, trailing song, which is often heard without the singer ever being seen. It's very common nationwide but prefers to stay hidden in the protection of a tree's foliage, and rarely ventures out into the open. It eats mostly insects and spiders off leaves and branches, and like the fantail, can hover for a few seconds to get at hard-to-reach prey. The materials for the nest — grasses, leaves, moss and spider webs — are gathered by the male bird, but the female does all the building work, and lines the insides with feathers and moss. The finished nest is a hanging pear-shaped affair, secured to branches, and with one very small side entrance. This gives it some protection from predators such as rats, but the shining cuckoo still sometimes manages to get in to lay its own eggs in the warbler's nest.

Grey warblers weigh around 6.5g and can live for about 10 years.

Kōkako

Now confined to forests in the central North Island, the rarely seen kōkako is very much a bird of the trees. It has small wings and doesn't fly much further than going from one tree to the next, or scuttling, running and flapping its way through the tree branches in search of food. It will even jump and glide to a distant branch.

It eats fresh leaves, flowers, small fruit and insects. It takes its food parrot-fashion — perching on one leg and clasping the food with the other foot. Slightly longer than the tūī and nearly twice its body weight, the Kōkako can live for about 20 years.

The skin folds at the base of the bill show that kōkako belongs to the wattlebird family, which includes the ground-feeding saddleback — tīeke — and the extinct huia. The bird's name comes from its call of *ko-ka-kooo*.

Silvereye — Pihipihi

This Australian bird was first seen in New Zealand in the early 1830s, and a large flock arrived in Waikenae, near Wellington, in 1856. It has since spread quickly throughout the country, and can be seen around trees in parks, gardens and forests, usually in small flocks. It has a brush-tipped tongue, like the tūī and the bellbird, and seeks out the same flowers for their nectar. It also eats fruit, spiders and insects such as aphids, caterpillars, flies and moths. Its small, cup-shaped nest is usually strung between small upright twigs or branches. Weighing just 18g and measuring 13cm, it's the smallest of the brush-tongued birds, although it can live for 11 years or more.

Kererū

New Zealand's native pigeon is common in forests nationwide. It's also known as kūkū, which is closer to its call of 'coo-coo'. It feeds on the leaves, fruit and flowers of many native trees, and especially likes the berries of nīkau, pūriri, miro, karaka, mataī and tawa. Many of these fruit are far too big for other birds to pluck and eat, but the kererū has the greatest gape of all our native birds, so can cope well, even with the orange 46mm-long karaka berries — one of the biggest of all. This makes the kererū a vital aid in the spread and survival of many of our native trees.

In spring and summer, kererū can be seen 'displaying' to find a mate. The bird flies steeply into the air above the trees, then stalls in flight before diving back down with wings held out stiffly.

It's one of our heaviest flying birds, often tipping the scales at 650g and it can live for over 20 years.

Now a protected bird, kererū were highly prized by early Māori — besides being big enough to provide a decent meal, the bird's feathers were used for making cloaks, and for decorating gourds.

Yellow-Crowned Parakeet — Kākāriki

This small parrot is the most common of several parakeet species found in New Zealand — the Māori name means both 'green' and 'small parrot'. Once there were flocks of thousands of parakeets, but predators, hunting and farming have reduced their numbers dramatically, and now they're only to be seen in forests in the central North Island, down to Wellington, and in some areas of the West Coast. They usually remain high in the trees, where they eat new leaves, buds, fruit, seeds and insects. They will sometimes forage on the forest floor for fallen berries. Some will chew the leaves of mānuka and kānuka, which contain chemicals that kill insects, and spread the juice through their feathers to control lice. They usually nest in the holes and crevices of old trees.

They weigh around 40–50g and are up to 25cm in length. Kākāriki can live for 5–7 years.

Twice the weight of the kākāriki is the very colourful Eastern Rosella, which escaped into the wild in 1910 and is now seen mostly in forests around Auckland and Northland, although there are small populations elsewhere, such as Wellington and Canterbury. They live in small groups and often nest in the holes of forest trees and in the trunks of tree ferns. They eat seeds, flowers, young shoots and insects. Like the kākāriki, they will occasionally forage on the ground. The rosella's call is a very distinctive *twink twink*. They can live for around 10 years.

Kākā

This large parrot lives in central and northern North Island forests, the Wellington region, and the West Coast of the South Island. It climbs through trees and branches monkey-style, walking and clambering with feet and bill. The kākā has a brush-tipped tongue, like tūī, so it takes nectar from flowers, but also seeks out insects, fruit and new leaves to eat. Its favourite foods are the grubs of insects hidden in tunnels under the tree bark, especially the grubs of the kānuka longhorn beetle (page 22). It will spend a long time tearing away bark with its long bill and sharp claws just to get at one grub.

While these birds prefer forests, they will forage in parks and gardens during winter to feed on other plants. The red feathers of the kākā were much prized by Māori, who used them to make the cloaks of chiefs, and for other decorations.

Nests are often made in the hollows and holes of old trees. Kākā can weigh over 500g, and can live for 20 years or more.

Morepork — Ruru

This small owl's call — sometimes described as *quor-quo*, sounded like *ruru* to Māori, but Europeans thought it was like *more-pork*. It's common nationwide — in parks, gardens and forests. During the day, it roosts in quiet spots in trees — old holes, or well-concealed forks in branches. After sunset, it flies out to capture beetles, moths and even small birds in flight, and also to pounce on any opportune ground prey, such as mice, rats and lizards.

It has excellent night vision, and its hearing is acute, as an owl's ear bones are asymmetric, this means that each side receives sound slightly differently, enabling the bird to target and 'zero-in' on prey in the near-dark precisely. And when it takes off from its perch, the ruru's flight is completely silent, thanks to the softer feathers on the edges of its wings, making it the perfect hunter.

The ruru is one of the very few birds that have benefitted from the arrival of humans and the introduction of animals such as rats, mice and small European birds. For this owl, it was just extra prey to hunt.

The ruru can live for about 6–10 years.

Little Shag — Kawaupaka

While some birds of shore and sea will occasionally nest in coastal trees, species of shag will sometimes nest in flocks of hundreds in trees by the water — especially pōhutukawa trees in the north. The most common is the little shag, found nationwide wherever there is water — lakes, rivers and estuaries — where it dives to take fish, frogs and freshwater crayfish. They can stay underwater for more than half a minute, and after several dives need to stand with wings outspread to dry out. The trees often suffer greatly from the birds' heavy landings, their sprawling untidy nests, and the large number of droppings. Weighing about 800g, this shag is the smallest of our species and can live for 6 years or more.

One of the fastest-growing native trees in New Zealand is the broadleaf — known as pāpāumu in the North Island, and as kāpuka in the South Island. It can grow 20–40cm a year, so is often planted and maintained as a hedging plant. In the wild, it can grow to 10m or more. It's a hardy species and does well in coastal areas as it tolerates salt from sea winds. Part of its Latin name — *littoralis* — means 'growing by the sea'.

Bats — Pekapeka

New Zealand is home to two bat species — the short-tailed and the long-tailed bat.

The long-tailed can be seen throughout most of the country, flying from its roosts at dusk to hunt for winged insects, which it takes in flight. It navigates in the air and detects flying insects — midges, beetles, mosquitoes and moths — by means of echolocation, emitting a series of audible 'clicks' as it does so. It can fly at speeds of up to 60k/ph. It uses several roosting places — in caves or deep boulder crevices, and in hollows and holes in living or dead trees, such as tōtara and mataī, and even in cabbage trees. In colder weather, the bats remain in their roosts half asleep in a state of torpor for several days or even weeks at a time, but become active again once the weather warms up. Although it has a wingspan of 25–28cm, the long-tailed bat weighs only about 8–12g. It can live for 11 years or more.

The short-tailed bat is the only bat in the world to forage for food on the forest floor, as well as hunting in the air like its long-tailed cousin. It 'walks' around on the ground using the joints of its folded wings as front limbs. It seeks out food such as fallen fruit, wētā, cockroaches, beetles and spiders. It uses similar roosts to its cousin — holes and hollows in larger trees. It's slightly larger than the long-tailed, with a wingspan of around 30cm, and can weigh about 16g. It can live for about 6–10 years. The short-tailed bat is comparatively rare and is now considered at risk.

60M
50M
40M
35M
30M
25M
20M
15M
10M
5M
2M
1. KŌWHAI
5. PUKATEA
7. KAHIKATEA
9. MATAĪ
10. MĀNUKA
2. REWAREWA
6. MIRO
11. TŌTARA
3. BEECH
1 KŌWHAI
Sophora microphylla/ S tetraptera 10–14m
2 REWAREWA
Knightia excelsa 30–40m
3 BEECH
Fuscospora/ Lophozonia sp 25–30m
4 NĪKAU
Rhopalostylis sapida 10m
5 PUKATEA
Laurelia novae-zelandiae 35m
6 MIRO
Prumnopitys ferruginea 25m
7 KAHIKATEA
Dacrycarpus dacrydioides 60m
8 CABBAGE TREE/ TĪ KŌUKA
Cordyline australis 10–20m
9 MATAĪ
Prumnopitys taxifolia 25–30m
10 MĀNUKA
Leptospermum scoparium 5–8m
11 TŌTAR
Podocarpu totara 25–3

PŪRIRI
15. KAWAKA
20. TAWA
22. TARAIRE
RIMU
16. PŌHUTUKAWA
21. MANGROVE
TĀNEKAHA
18. KAURI
60M
50M
40M
35M
30M
25M
20M
15M
10M
5M
2M
KAIRARU
Kairaru was the greatest kauri tree to have been officially measured before its destruction by fire in the late 19th century. It was about 4000 years old.
13 RIMU
Dacrydium cupressinum 20–40m
15 KAWAKAWA/ NZ CEDAR
Libocedrus plumosa 25m
17 PŌNGA/ SILVER FERN
Cyathea dealbata 10m
18 KAURI
Agathis australis 25–50m
21 MANGROVE/MĀNAWA
Avicennia marina australasica 5–15m
PŪRIRI
x lucens
14 TĀNEKAHA
Phyllocladus trichomanoides 20–25m
16 PŌHUTUKAWA
Metrosideros excelsa 10–20m
19 MAMAKU
Cyathea medullaris 10–20m
20 TAWA
Beilschmiedia tawa 25m
22 TARAIRE
Beilschmiedia tarairi 20–22m

INDEX